A Guided Walk round St Andre

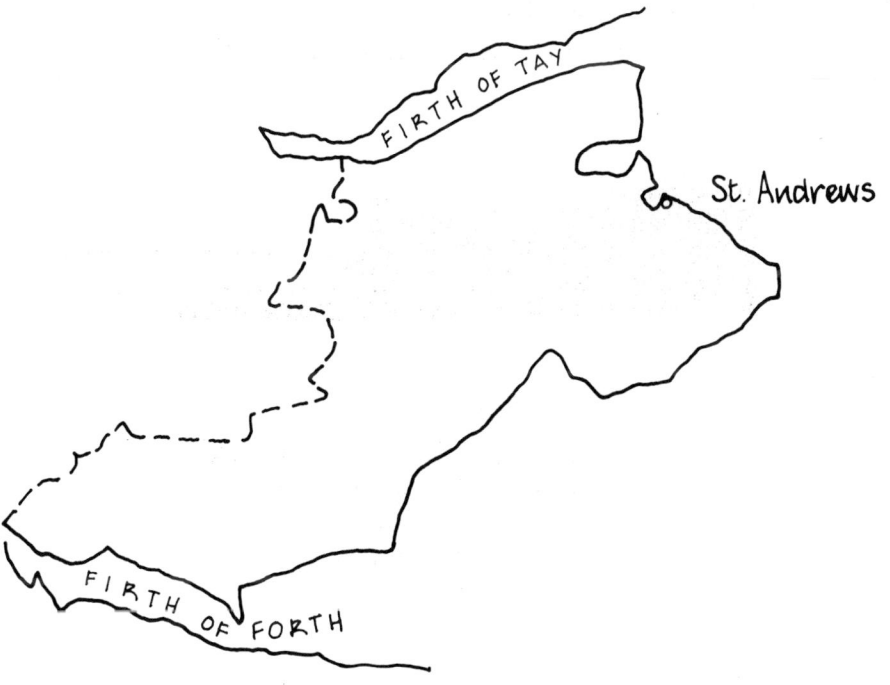

FIRTH OF TAY

St. Andrews

FIRTH OF FORTH

The Kingdom of Fife

The first edition of this book was printed in April, 1990.

Second Revised Edition – April, 1992
ISBN 0-9519134-1-7

Third Revised Edition – May, 1996

The paper for this third revised edition was supplied by

TULLIS RUSSELL
MARKINCH
FIFE

Text handwritten and illustrations by John M. Pearson
© Copyright J.M.P. All rights reserved 1996
A catalogue record for this book is available
from the British Library ISBN 0-9519134-9-2

Printed by:-
Levenmouth Printers,
Banbeath Place,
Leven, Fife.

A Guided Walk round St. Andrews

by John M. Pearson

CONTENTS

Acknowledgements   5
Introduction   6

Bibliography   63
The Author   64

ILLUSTRATIONS

Kirkhill from the harbour	6
St. Rules Tower	7
The harbour	9
The Mill Port	10
Entrance to St. Leonards	11
Deans Court from the Pends	12
The ruined Cathedral	13
The Cathedral and St. Rules Tower	14
North Street	15
Foretower of the Castle	16
The Castle	17
Cobbled initials of George Wishart	18
St. Salvator's College	19
St. Salvator's Tower	20
Entry to St. Salvator's College	21
Bishop Kennedy's Tomb	22
Bell Tower – St. Mary's College	23
24 College Street	24
East end of Market Street	25
A.T. Hoggs Ltd	26
St. Salvators Hall	27
Playfair Terrace	28
Martyrs Monument	29
Royal and Ancient Clubhouse	30
Swilken Bridge & Old Course	32
Auchterlonies	34
Abbotsford Crescent	35
The Pancake Place	36
The West Port	37
Louden's Close	38
Alison's Close	39
Ladebraes Walk	40
Blackfriars Chapel	41
Burgher Close	42
The Town Kirk	43,44
Town Hall	46
Polish mosaic	47
J & G Innes Ltd	48
Logie's Lane	49
College Street	50
Fountain in Market Street	51
Crails Lane	52
St. Mary's College	53,54
The Doocot	55
71, South Street	56
South Court	57
The Byre Theatre	58
South Court	59
The Roundel	60
Deans Court	61
Kirkhill	62

MAPS

Town map in mid-19th century	8
Kirkhill – Millport	9
Millport – The Pends	10
The Pends – Cathedral	12
Cathedral – Castle	15
Castle – North Street	20
North Street – Market Street	25
Muttoes Lane – North Street	26
North Street – The Scores	28
Golf Place – The Links	30
Golf Place – West Port	37
West Port – Ladebraes Walk	39
Ladebraes Walk – South Street	41
South Street – Town Kirk	42
Logie's Lane – Market Street	45
Market Street – South Street	52
St. Mary's College	55
South Street – South Court	57
Byre Theatre – South Street	60
Deans Court – Kirkhill	62
Map of St. Andrews – Back Cover	

ACKNOWLEDGEMENTS

'A rouch Scots blanket wi' a fringe o' gowd'

- so James V described the Kingdom of Fife and even today the jewel in that fringe of gold is still undoubtably St. Andrews.

It was an interesting and educational venture to produce this book on St. Andrews and I am grateful for all the advice and encouragement offered by friends and family - especially my parents - Tom and Betty Pearson.

St. Andrews continues to stand the test of time and little has changed since the first edition was published in 1990. This third revised edition, however, includes new sketches of the Town Kirk, Town Hall and St. Salvators Hall.

I am also grateful for assistance given by local businesses - Auchterlonies, A.T. Hoggs Ltd., J & G Innes Ltd, The Pancake Place and Tullis Russell of Markinch.

Finally I acknowledge that the street map on the back cover is based on the O.S. map of St. Andrews with permission of H.M.S.O.(c)

John M. Pearson

5

1. Looking towards Kirkhill from the harbour

INTRODUCTION

In his praise of the Royal Air Force during the Battle of Britain Sir Winston Churchill stated that "Never in the field of human conflict was so much owed by so many to so few." In a slightly different context never has Scotland owed so much to one particular town for its influence in national affairs. That town is St. Andrews - a town that has played a major role in the development of Scottish religious history, Scottish education and the international world of golf.

St. Andrews was founded on the legend that the bones of the Apostle, St. Andrew, were brought to the old township of Kilrymont over 1000 years ago. As a result pilgrims flocked from all over Europe to worship the remains of St. Andrew - the Patron Saint of Scotland.

From these early days religion was a strong influence in the development of St. Andrews. First of all the Celtic Church was founded by the Culdees on Kirkhill, then the Church of St. Rule, followed by the Cathedral in 1160. This was a major step in establishing St. Andrews as a force in Scottish religious and political circles.

During these troubled times the Castle was built about 1200 and formed both Fortress and Palace for the Bishops.

The Church always placed a great emphasis on education and consequently was instrumental in establishing the University in St. Andrews between 1410-1414. This was the first University in all Scotland and later development included the founding of St. Salvator's College in 1450, St. Leonard's College in 1512 and St. Mary's College in 1537.

The Reformation in 1559 was to signal the end of St. Andrews as a dominant religious force in Scotland. Consequently both the Castle and Cathedral gradually declined in importance and eventually fell into ruin.

"As one door shuts, another opens" and with the decline of religion the importance of St. Andrews was kept to the fore by the University and then by the Game of Golf. In 1754 the Society of St. Andrews Golfers was formed and with the blessing of a Royal Patron in 1834 became known as the Royal and Ancient Golf Club. Ever since, golf has flourished and the Royal and Ancient is now recognised internationally as the Home of Golf.

2. St. Rule's Tower

Even today much of the turbulent history of St. Andrews may still be appreciated. The medieval street plan still exists and many of the buildings which contribute to the character and heritage of the town still remain.

From early times settlement was concentrated around the harbour and extended as far as the present line of North and South Castle Street. By medieval times greater prosperity, an increased population and the importance of St. Andrews as the ecclesiastical centre of Scotland all contributed to the expansion of the city. Development took place along and between the four main streets — North St., South St., Market St. and the Scores, formerly known as the Swallowgait.

The land between these streets was divided into 10 metre wide strips with buildings situated on the street front. Access to the rear was through a pend, and other buildings extended back from the street at right angles, thus forming a close or narrow street. This type of development was a significant factor in forming the character of St. Andrews.

Entry into the old city was gained through gates or ports located at strategic points. These ports formed a control point for trade and merchandise into and out of St. Andrews, and today the only surviving port is the West Port. Ever since Provost Sir Hugh Lyon Playfair undertook to improve the city in the mid-nineteenth century there has been a conscious effort to preserve the heritage of St. Andrews. Consequently this provides a great opportunity to explore St. Andrews on foot and relive the colourful history of a truly great city in the ancient Kingdom of Fife. *∞*

STREET PLAN OF ST. ANDREWS IN THE MID-NINETEENTH CENTURY.

3. The harbour

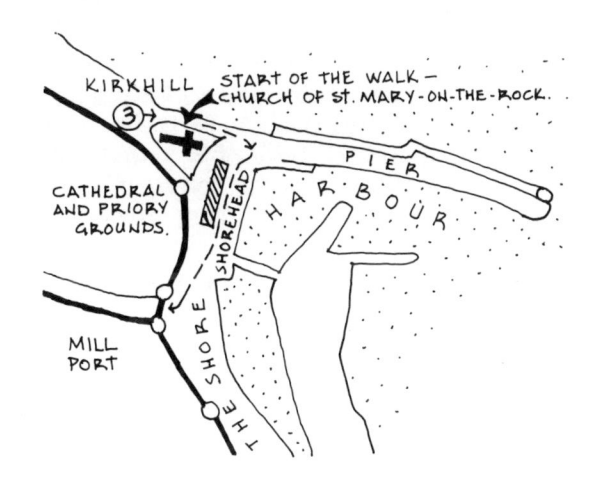

Our walk starts on Kirkhill, formerly known as Kirk Heugh, where the foundations of the twelfth century Culdee Church of St. Mary-on-the-Rock are all that remain of an ancient religious order. Legend indicates that the first Culdee Church was built on a Rock beyond the end of the present pier. About the sixth century, however, a rising sea level forced the Culdees to rebuild on the Kirkhill. The existence of this Church lay forgotten until 1860 when excavations for a gun battery exposed the stone foundations as we see them today.

Continue on down Kirkhill to the harbour which was previously a vital sea link for trade with the continent up until the 1700's. Sea trade was badly affected because St. Andrews suffered a decline in importance due to the Reformation and subsequent events. Even so the harbour was not allowed to fall into neglect and the pier was rebuilt and strengthened with stones taken from the Castle and Cathedral.

The pier features in University folklore and on Sundays after chapel the University students, resplendent in their vivid red gowns, embark on their traditional walk along the pier.

9

We now follow "The shore" by the harbour until we reach the Mill Port - a massive stone gateway which leads us through to Pends Road. The Mill Port is one of the three surviving gateways in the six metre high Precinct Wall which surrounded the Priory. There are also thirteen of the original sixteen towers still standing. Many of the plaques on the towers depict the arms of Prior John Hepburn who was responsible for strengthening and increasing the height of the Priory Wall in the early sixteenth century. The largest of these towers is the Haunted Tower and after being sealed for many years it was secretly opened in 1868. Inside were found many bones, the coffins of victims of the plague in 1605 and the perfectly preserved body of a young lady wearing white, leather gloves. Today it is only the Ghost of the White Lady that survives.

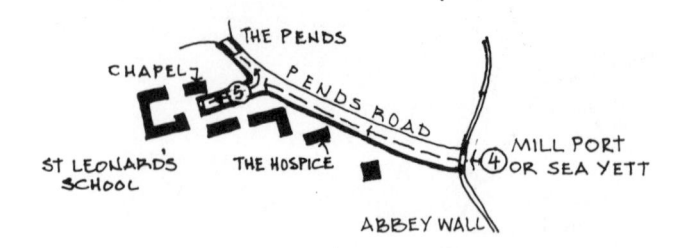

4. The Mill Port

Carry on through the Mill Port and plod on uphill alongside this towering stone wall with its old decorative street lamps. As we near the bend in Pends Road the approach to St. Leonards School and Chapel is framed by the high stone walls and the overhanging avenue of trees. In the early twelfth century this was the site of St. Leonards Hospice which provided shelter for the pilgrims visiting the shrine of St. Andrew. In 1512 the buildings were founded by Archbishop Alexander Stewart and Prior John Hepburn to form part of the University.

On entering the Courtyard St. Leonards Chapel is to our right. After falling into disrepair the Chapel was restored in the early 1900's and is still used today as a Chapel by the University. The other building, on the same side of the courtyard, is the Hall which was rebuilt in the eighteenth century. Apart from the Chapel, all the buildings form St. Leonards School which was founded in 1877 to provide educational facilities for women.

5. Entrance to St. Leonards

6. Deans Court from the Pends

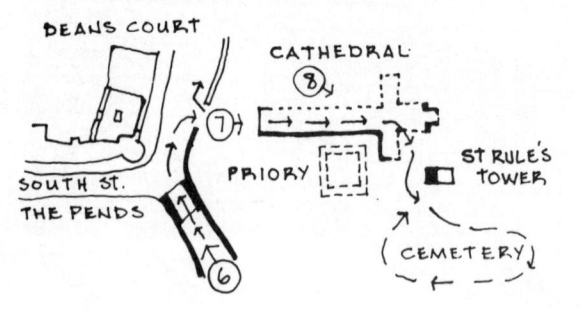

Retracing our steps to Pends Road we then pass through the Pends - a fourteenth century vaulted gatehouse which formed the main entrance to the Priory. Over on the left is Deans Court, which we will visit later, and to our right is the ruined Cathedral Church of St. Andrews. The nineteen metre high ruins of the east and west gables help to capture the scale of what was once the largest, longest and greatest Cathedral in all Scotland. Internally it measured 109 metres long by nineteen metres wide across the Nave.

The founding of the Cathedral and Priory was a major step in establishing St. Andrews as an ecclesiastical centre which played a dominant part in Scottish religious history. Both the Cathedral and Priory succeeded the nearby Church of St. Rule and the Church of St. Mary-on-the-Rock. The Culdees, who worshipped in the latter, were a separate religious order from the Cathedral but by the fourteenth century their power and presence had all but disappeared.

St. Andrews Cathedral performed two functions as it was not only the Cathedral Church of the diocese of St. Andrews but also the Church of the Augustinian Order of Canons who occupied the adjacent Priory to the south of the Cathedral.

12

Founded in 1160 the Cathedral was consecrated by Bishop Lamberton in 1318, in an illustrious company which included King Robert the Bruce - hero of Bannockburn.

Down through the centuries the Cathedral was witness to many Scottish historical events. These included the marriage of King James V to the French Queen Mary de Guise in 1538 and the cruel convictions of the Protestant martyrs Patrick Hamilton, George Wishart and Walter Myln. In 1472 St. Andrews was elevated to the dignatory of an archepiscopal and metropolitan see. Shortly after, in 1487, the Pope made the Cathedral into the Seat of the Primate of All Scotland.

At the height of the Reformation in June 1559 the Cathedral was sacked by followers of the Reformer John Knox. His fiery sermon in the Town Kirk - the Holy Trinity Church - reputedly sparked off the riot amongst the congregation. The looting of the Cathedral and other religious buildings, however, may well have been an organised wave of crime as many of the priceless treasures that decorated these buildings simply disappeared.

Apart from the outline of the Priory foundations little remains of the Priory buildings which were designed around a cloister to the south wall of the Cathedral.

7. The ruined Cathedral

8. East end of the Cathedral and St. Rule's Tower

Beyond the east gable wall of the Cathedral stands the intriguing Church of St. Regulus or St. Rule. Although it preceded the Cathedral no one has accurately pinpointed the founding date of this Church. It has been associated with the arrival of St. Rule with the bones of the Apostle Andrew in possibly the eighth or ninth century. Yet others have dated it about 1127-44 because the tower displays many architectural features incorporated in the twelfth century Church of Wharram-le-Street in Yorkshire. In the Chapel is a monument to Dr. Thomas Chalmers (1780-1847), Professor of Mathematics in St. Andrews and of Divinity in Edinburgh and subsequently the First Moderator of the General Assembly of the Free Church of Scotland.

Within the shadows of the Cathedral lie many generations of St. Andrews citizens. They include father and son Tom Morris - the famous golfers - and also Willie Auchterlonie who was the last St. Andrews man to win the prized Open Golf Championship in 1893.

Over in the Eastern Cemetery is the Holy Well where the monks drew their fresh water. Among the many monuments are ones to Colonel Aitken for his role in the defence of Lucknow in 1857 and to the crew of the Merlin who were all drowned when their ship was wrecked off St. Andrews in 1881. Andrew Lang, the scholar, poet and writer of St. Andrews also lies buried here.

9. North Street

Leaving the Cathedral and Priory Precinct we now head for the Castle which was the main residence and fortress for the Bishops of St. Andrews. In North Street the St. Andrews Preservation Trust Museum is to our left at no 12 and on our right are a row of two storey pantiled houses. No 19 is of particular interest with its stone forestair supported by a corner pillar. In the middle distance is the spire of St. Salvators College.

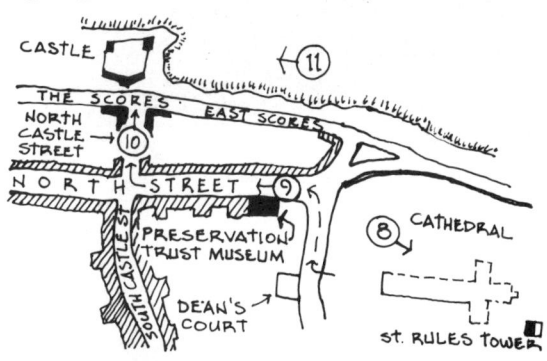

15

Turn right into North Castle Street, formerly known as Castle Wynd and Fishergate. On our right are the old houses of the street and on the left, Castle Wynd House and All Saints Church. At the end of the street are the towering remains of the large fore-tower of the Castle. Although the Castle ruins that are still standing today date mainly from the sixteenth century the original Castle was built by Bishop Roger about 1200. During the Wars of Independence in the early 1300's when Scotland was fighting for its very survival from English dominance, the Castle was destroyed and rebuilt several times.

The history of the Castle is a cruel one and reflects desperate times in medieval Scotland. In the north west corner is the ruined Sea Tower which holds the prisons and the infamous Bottle Dungeon. A circular opening in the floor allows access to the Bottle Dungeon which is aptly named due to its bottle shape carved out of the rock below. The dungeon is 4½ metres across at the base and is 7½ metres deep. It's dark, dank interior is a reminder of a cruel and horrid past.

Among the many people who were imprisoned here were Patrick Hamilton, Walter Myln, George Wishart and John Roger, a Black Friar, who was murdered in the dark depths of the dungeon before being thrown over the cliffs.

10. The fore-tower of the Castle

11. The Castle

Besides the Bottle Dungeon the other major attractions are the mines and countermines which demonstrate the medieval techniques employed during sieges. The mines that were discovered here were dug out during the siege of 1546-47. The entrance to the mine which was dug out by the attackers is located in the modern house on the corner of Castle Wynd. In order to counter this mine the defending Protestant forces succeeded in tunnelling outwards and breaking down into the advancing tunnel. This foiled the attacking forces from undermining the Castle fortifications.

17

Outside the Castle the initials of George Wishart are marked in the roadway. This was the spot where he was burnt to death in 1546 as Cardinal Beaton watched from a Castle window. Shortly after the death of Wishart the Cardinal was murdered in revenge. A small group of Protestants gained entry into the Castle by mingling with the masons who were employed to strengthen the Castle defences. Quickly taking the garrison by surprise they took control of the Castle. Before long the body of the Cardinal hung from the very window where he witnessed Wishart burning at the stake.

The Protestant forces, with the aid of Henry VIII of England held out under siege for over twelve months. In June 1547 the arrival of the French fleet forced a hasty surrender as the Castle was bombarded by cannon from land and sea by the combined forces of the Auld Alliance. Among the Protestants led away to the galleys was a certain John Knox who was to play a major part in establishing the Protestant religion in Scotland.

The successor to Cardinal Beaton was the Archbishop John Hamilton who rebuilt the Castle. His coat of arms is still visible on the Fore Tower between the two large windows. The Archbishop was also to play a major role in establishing St. Marys College as part of the St. Andrews University complex.

The next one hundred years history of the Castle passed without too much mishap. With the decline of the Catholic Church the ownership of the Castle was temporarily transferred to the Crown in 1587; then to the Earl of Dunbar and then back again in 1612 to the Church. By 1654 the Castle stood in ruins and the Town Council chose to demolish the Castle Walls and use the stone for repairing the pier and harbour walls. Today the Castle, Cathedral and Priory are held in trust for the Nation by the Secretary of State for Scotland.

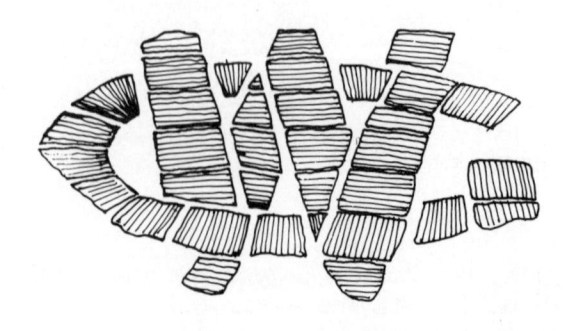

Cobbled initials of George Wishart

Our walk continues down the Scores, formerly known as Swallowgait and which had town ports located at either end. Before that this street was known as Castlegate. Over to our right are several eyecatching Victorian buildings while to our left is the St. Salvator College.

Turning left up Butts Wynd - the street which originally gave access to the Bow Butts where archery practice took place - we see straight through to South Street in the far distance. On the corner of Market Street the splayed corbelled gable stands out providing some interest to the street scene.

At the end of Butts Wynd we are now below the impressive Tower of St. Salvator with its Church and College. Before entering into the College Grounds look for the intertwined initials of Patrick Hamilton set out in the cobbles. As the plaque on the nearby wall informs us Patrick Hamilton was accused of heresy and his slow cruel death at the stake in February 1528 made him Scotland's first martyr in the Reformation. According to folklore the face of Patrick Hamilton is supposedly etched into the stone work over the archway.

12. Entrance to St. Salvators College with the initials of Patrick Hamilton in the foreground.

19

Originally the tower had no steeple and it was from here that the French had bombarded the Castle into submission with their cannon positioned on top of the tower in 1546. The spire was built on the instruction of Archbishop John Hamilton in 1550 and contains the original bells of the College. The bells are named as 'Kate Kennedy' or 'Katherine' and that of St. Leonard's College as 'Elizabeth', although both bells have now been recast.

The North Street frontage of both St. Salvators Tower and Church survive from medieval times and are a splendid monument to the aspirations and achievements of Bishop James Kennedy who lies entombed within the Church.

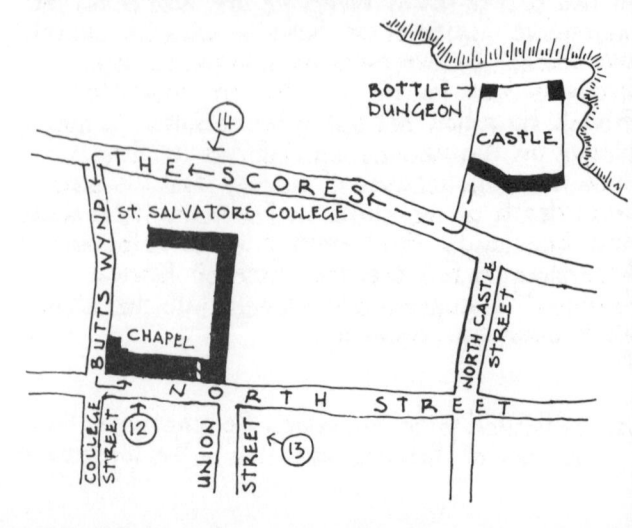

13. St. Salvator's Tower

The creation of the University was due to the role of the Culdees on Kirkhill, and latterly the Augustinian Order at the Priory, who would have organised the tuition and studying of the gospels. With the backing of Bishop Henry Wardlaw the Priors founded a school for higher studies in 1410. The constitution was based on that of Orleans University in France and by 1414 the necessary Papal Bulls had been granted from Rome. This confirmed the formation of St. Andrews University — the first University in all Scotland.

Temporary accommodation was initially acquired for the Faculty of Theology and Arts on the site of what is now the University Library in South Street. By 1430 the Pedagogy was founded on an adjoining site to hold the Faculty of Arts. Both these faculties were eventually absorbed into St. Mary's College which was founded in 1537.

The first University buildings to be erected were the College and Church of St. Salvator which were founded in 1450 by Bishop James Kennedy — renowned as one of the great Scotsmen of his era.

In 1747 St. Salvator's College amalgamated with St. Leonard's College to form United Colleges.

14. Entry to St. Salvator's College from the Scores

15. Bishop Kennedy's tomb

The medieval Collegiate Church at St. Salvator is still the main centre for academic worship in St. Andrews and within the Chapel is the tomb of Bishop Kennedy. In the late nineteenth century the original vaulted Chapel roof was considered dangerous and uncermoniously demolished. The whole roof was brought down within the walls causing great damage to the interior and especially to the Bishop's tomb. Besides the famous tomb other memorials include one to Andrew Lang, the poet and historian who based much of his verse on his student days at the University. There is also John Knox's Pulpit and this may well be the pulpit from where Knox preached his famous sermon at Holy Trinity Church.

In the vestry is the College mace presented by Bishop Kennedy in 1461. There are two older maces belonging to the Faculties of Arts and Canon Law along with three modern maces presented to the University this century. The oldest object in the University, however, is the matrix of the University Seal dating back before 1418.

In 1826 an investigation was carried out by the Royal Commission into the running of the University. This resulted in the reconstruction of all the University buildings and the introduction of a new teaching curriculum.

This was followed by sweeping changes in administration with implementation of the Act of 1858. By 1876, however, the University was lurching in the Doldrums as the number of students dropped dramatically to a mere 130. When a recruiting drive achieved limited success the University took the unprecedented step of encouraging women to enrol as students. By 1892 the University Hall was established as a residence for women and this positive step had once again proved St. Andrews University as one of the leaders in the field of education.

About this time the nearby City of Dundee was thriving with all the benefits of the industrial revolution. Consequently many an envious eye was cast at St. Andrews with its University and therefore, it was no surprise when the University College of Dundee was founded in 1881. Nearly a century later Dundee achieved full University status in 1967. This resulted in St. Andrews conceding the Faculties of Medicine and Law and left the University in a precarious position. In order to survive this loss new Chairs were established to justify the existence of the University. This required a massive building programme throughout St. Andrews to provide new student accommodation and educational facilities. All these developments proved to be a success and the University has benefited immensely.

16. The Bell Tower and the old thorn tree at St. Mary's College.

Burgh Coat of Arms

17. No 24 College Street

St. Andrews University is steeped in tradition and one of the most popular is the Kate Kennedy pageant. Although the origins may well date back to the early fifteenth century the students established an end of term celebration in 1849 that eventually blossomed into the pageant as it is today. In 1874 the pageant was banned because of unruly and drunken behaviour and it was not revived until 1926 when the Kate Kennedy Club was formed.

Today the pageant takes the form of a procession through the streets of St. Andrews with all the famous characters of yesteryear represented. The main character is the first year male student who masquerades as Kate Kennedy - the niece of the founder of St. Salvators College - Bishop James Kennedy. The procession is led by St. Andrew, to the toll of Kate's Bell, from St Salvators College, along North Street to the Castle, then down the Scores and into Market Street, then on to the West Port before returning to the Quadrangle via the Cathedral.

It is a colourful, lively procession which features many people who were involved in the history of both St. Andrews and Scotland. It also gives enjoyment to both the Town and Gown and is now firmly established in the calendar of events of St. Andrews.

On leaving St. Salvators College we cross over to College Street which typifies the traditional type housing of old St. Andrews. The corner house at no 24 is a good example with its pantiled roof, crow stepped gable, stone walls and forestair. At the end of College Street, formerly Bucklers Wynd, we enter the cobbled Market Street, the main commercial centre of medieval St. Andrews.

Besides the weekly markets various Royal decrees had granted permission for trading markets dating back to 1153 in the reign of King Malcolm. Originally there were five annual markets but only the Lammas Market survives today and consequently is the oldest surviving medieval market in Scotland. It is held on the Lammas Tide or 1st of August and although its main purpose was for trading it eventually lapsed into an employment market for farmers looking for agricultural labour.

Gradually the Lammas Market became more of a fun fair with amusement stalls and sideshows, and this is the form it takes today as the Fair spills over into the streets of the town. Of the other four markets that have long since disappeared, the Senzie Market, held on the ninth day after Easter, was perhaps the most famous. It lasted for two weeks and people from all over Europe flocked to St. Andrews for the fair and festivities.

18. The East end of Market Street.

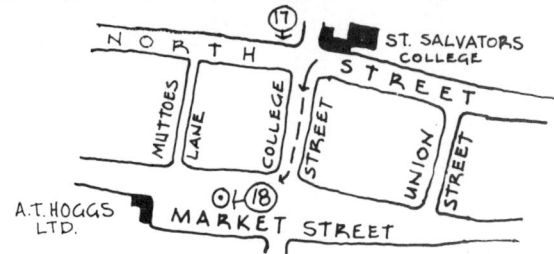

25

We will visit Market Street again so let us slip away down Muttoes Lane into North Street. All the three main streets are linked with these closes which add to the character of the town. On reaching North Street we turn left, then left again into Mercat Wynd and through an indoor shopping centre which leads us back into Market Street. Continue on down the street to the main intersection at Bell Street and Greyfriars Garden. These two streets were originally classified as Bell Street and formed part of a planning policy to link up the three main streets. — North Street, Market Street and South Street. Bell Street was named after the founder of Madras College which is the local secondary school. Greyfriars Garden was formed in 1836 and was named after the old Greyfriars ground through which the street passes.

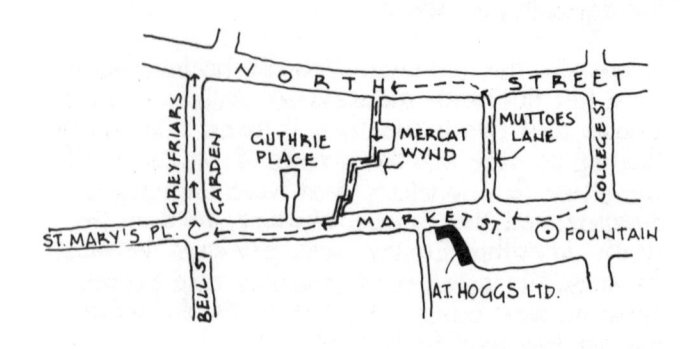

Hoggs
'Fife Footwear Co.
Established 1888
90, MARKET STREET, ST. ANDREWS

We now turn right into Greyfriars Garden which has a feeling of spaciousness created by the houses on the one side of the street and their gardens on the other. On reaching North Street turn left, and across the road we see further evidence of nineteenth century expansion. This included the building of Playfair Terrace and Pilmuir Place. The former was built in 1846 and named after Sir Hugh Lyon Playfair, the Provost of St. Andrews from 1842-1861.

In the early eighteen hundreds St. Andrews suffered greatly from neglect with its inadequate sewer system, foul smelling middens, uneven pavements and dilapidated buildings. All this changed with the appointment of Major Playfair as Provost in 1842. Previously the Major had gained considerable military expertise in India and he now turned his talents to leading a campaign of improvements to St. Andrews. Initially this involved the local citizens in raising funds to finances the various projects and this sparked a resurgence of interest in the town. As well as carrying out extensive improvements to practically every part of St. Andrews that we will visit on our walk, the Major was also instrumental in encouraging the Railways to build a branch line from Leuchars Junction. In 1856 Queen Victoria rewarded the Major with a knighthood for his achievements in St. Andrews.

St. Salvator's Hall

19. Playfair Terrace

Crossing over North Street we now slip down Gillespie Wynd which takes us between the high stone walls of the back gardens of Playfair and Gillespie Terrace. A left, then right turn and we catch a glimpse of the North Sea between the gables of the houses ahead.

On arriving at the Scores the tall, but simple Martyrs Monument stands opposite to commemorate the martyrs - Patrick Hamilton, Henry Forrest, George Wishart and Walter Myln - who are listed on the memorial. Only Paul Craw who was burned to death about a century before the rest is not mentioned. This area below is known as the Bow Butts where archers in medieval times would practise their skills which were vital to the defence of the nation. This custom prevailed well into the eighteenth century and was encouraged by the University which held their own archery competitions. One particular competition for the Silver Arrow and Medals dates from 1618 and famous winners include James, Marquis of Montrose in 1628. Ten years later he was instrumental in the signing of the National Covenant in Greyfriars Churchyard in Edinburgh. This was a document designed to uphold the Presbyterian form of Church Government in Scotland.

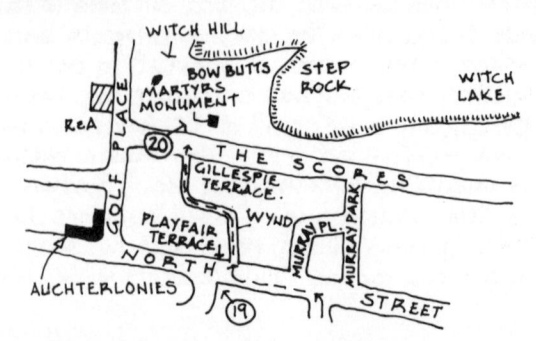

Wandering over to the edge of the cliffs we are now standing above the Step Rock Swimming Pool huddled into the cliff face. It is the ideal place for any hardy swimmer to take an invigorating dip in the refreshing waters of the North Sea. Yet in the distant past this area was not associated with fun and leisure.

In the aftermath of the Reformation in 1559 men and women accused of witchcraft were thrown into Witch Lake to our right to prove their innocence. It was not a fair trial because if the victims swam they were taken away to be burnt at the stake on Witch Hill near the Bow Butts.

This evil persecution was carried out with an intense zeal by the bigots of the new religious order. From 1569 until 1705, when the last witch was put to death in Market Street, these bigots pursued people suspected of witchcraft, either for political means or merely through ignorant superstitions. It was not until 1735, however, that the Scottish Witch Statutes were repealed and thus ended an unnecessary barbaric practice.

20. Martyrs' Monument

From our viewpoint on the cliffs the West Sands sweep round St. Andrews Bay and behind them are the world famous golfing links. This was always a barren area of land, totally inadequate for cultivation or grazing and it only provided turf sods to roof the houses of the poor. It made, however, for the ideal golf course and has hardly changed over the years.

Golf or 'gowf' as it is affectionately known has been associated with St. Andrews for hundreds of years. The earliest reference to golf in Scotland was in 1457 when James II outlawed the playing of golf and football so that men may concentrate on their archery skills — " Gowf and fitba to be utterly cryit doon and not usit."

The popularity of golf in St. Andrews eventually called for some form of framework to control the evolution of the game and this was achieved by the formation of the Society of St. Andrews Golfers on 14th May, 1754. The Society organised 'a course' comprising of nine holes out and nine holes back, with greens for putting the golf ball into the hole, and this forms the basis of the game played today. They also organised an annual competition to play for a Silver Club with the winner being elected Captain.

21. The Royal and Ancient Clubhouse

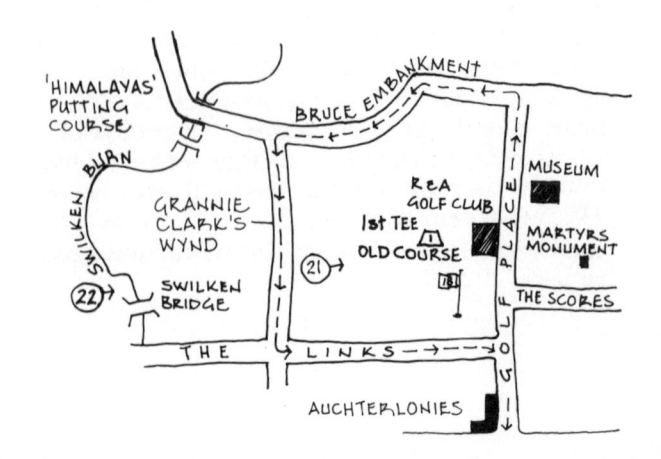

The game of golf had always attracted the keen attention of landowners and nobility and even Royalty were enthusiastic participants. In 1834 William IV was nominated as Patron of the Society and consequently the club name was changed to the Royal and Ancient Golf Club of St. Andrews. It is an impressive title which was instrumental in establishing St. Andrews as the Home of Golf. By 1854 the R & A, as it is often known, had built a new clubhouse which still survives today and is internationally known throughout the golfing world as the Headquarters of Golf.

In later years the Captain was elected to this prestigous post of the R & A and today tradition demands that he plays himself into office with a drive off the first tee. The first caddie to return the ball receives a gold sovereign from the Captain.

There are five golf courses on the links of St. Andrews - the 72 par Old Course where the Open Championships are played; the New Course (1895), the Jubilee (1897), the Eden (1914), the new 18 hole Strathtyrum Course which opened in 1993 and the 9 hole Balgove Course. Until 1946 the residents of St. Andrews had the privilege of playing over the Old Course free of charge, but since then an annual subscription has been charged.

With the rising importance of golf in St. Andrews it was only natural that firms should become involved in the manufacture of golf clubs. Down through the ages famous names such as Forgan, Auchterlonie and Anderson, and more recently J. B. Halley & Co. Ltd and the Swilken Golf Co. Ltd have all played their part in manufacturing clubs.

One of the early acceptable golf balls was the 'featherie' - quite simply a leather sphere crammed with a top hat of boiled feathers. The featherie was eventually replaced in the 1840's by the gutta percha. This ball was the brainwave of Robert Paterson, a native of St. Andrews, and it was mainly composed of the sap from Malaysian trees. By 1899, however, a rubbercored golf ball was introduced and this type of ball is still in use today.

Open Golf Championship Trophy

ST. ANDREWS LINKS

Descending to Golf Place we follow the road round into Bruce embankment and past the new R & A golf museum on our right. Ahead of us lies the Ladies Putting Green – a testing eighteen holes known locally as the Himalayas. We now turn left into Grannie Clarks Wynd which crosses the first and eighteenth fairways of the famous Old Course. This is the scene which greets the contenders for the Open Golf Championship. Thronged by huge crowds that gather round the eighteenth green and fairway the R & A Clubhouse has witnessed many a dramatic moment.

The first ever Golf Open was held at Prestwick, Ayrshire in 1860 and was won by Willie Park. The following year Tom Morris Senior from St. Andrews won the Open and then succeeded in retaining the title the next year in 1862. Further successes were recorded in 1864 and 1867 but in 1868 it was Tom Morris Junior who recorded his first Championship win at the age of seventeen.

22. The Swilken Bridge leading onto the 18th fairway of the

Tom Morris Junior went on to win the title in 1869, '70 and '72 and as there was no championship in 1871 he still holds a unique record of four consecutive victories. Although he died, aged twenty four he undoubtably remains as one of golf's greatest legends.

The first ever Open Golf Championship to be held at St. Andrews was in 1873. Even today the Old Course is still renowned for its seven immense double greens which are as challenging as the numerous bunkers which pepper the course. The names of many of the bunkers conjure up the hazards facing the golfers who are unfortunate enough to encounter them — Lions Mouth, Hell Bunker, Coffin Bunkers and Road Bunker to name but a few.

At the end of the 'wynd' turn left up The Links where the town and ladies golf clubs are situated overlooking the Old Course. At the top of the road turn right along Golf Place.

Course

Auchterlonies of St. Andrews

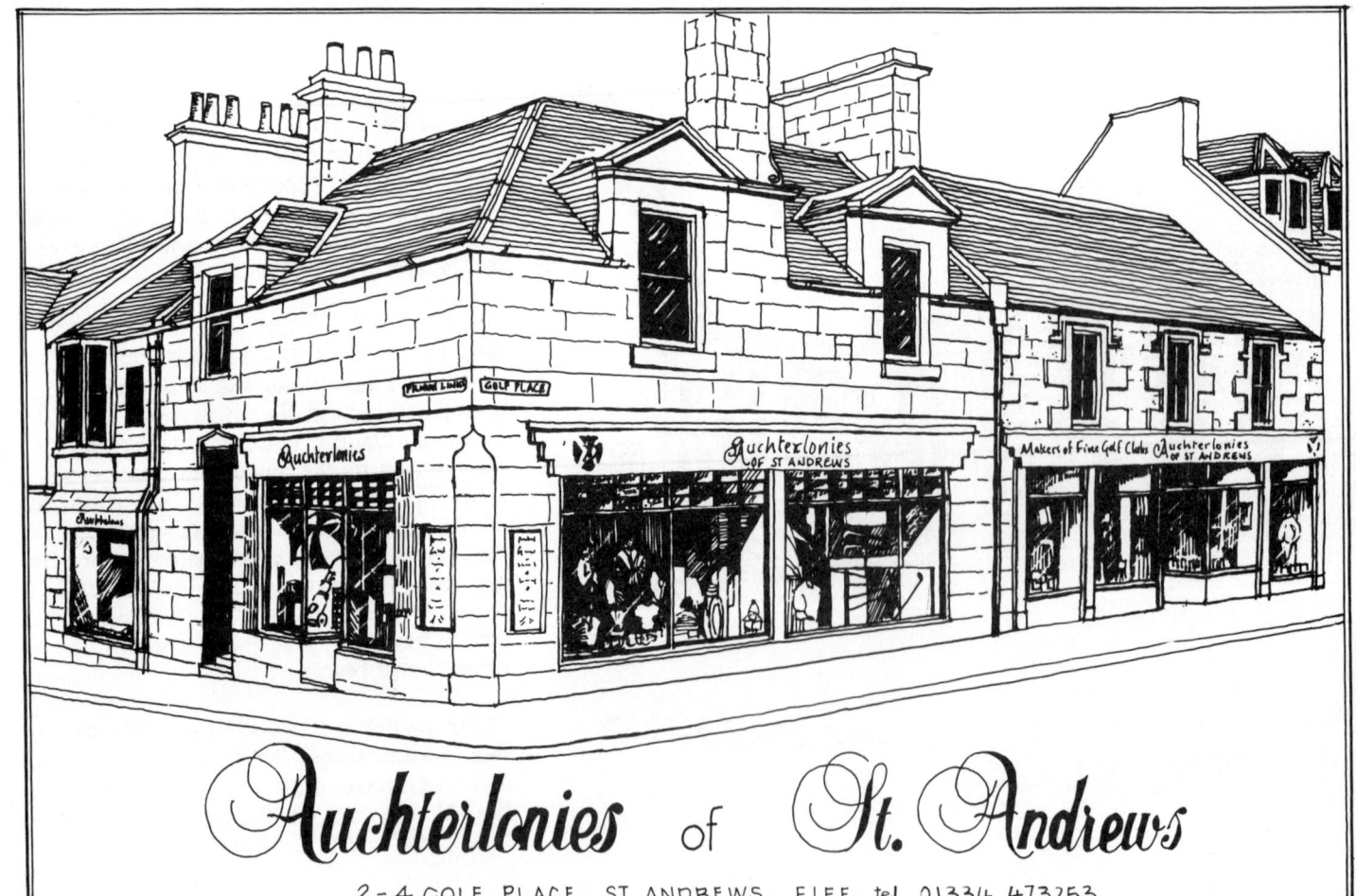

2-4 GOLF PLACE, ST. ANDREWS, FIFE. tel. 01334 473253
WHERE EVERYTHING FOR THE DISCERNING GOLFER IS TO BE FOUND

The Auchterlonie family have long been associated with golf. David Auchterlonie had six sons of whom Laurence, David, Willie and Tom were to make a name for themselves in golfing circles. Laurence won the U.S. Open Championship in 1902, David and Willie established the first Auchterlonie golf club manufacturing business and by 1919 Tom had also set up his own golf club business. Eventually competition from larger golf firms, who could mass produce clubs at very economical prices, forced David and Willie out of business in the 1930's. Tom and Eric survived by building up a successful retail side to the business. They also benefited from specialising in the manufacture of hand-made clubs - especially their woodenhead putter. Eric retired in 1986 thus ending nearly a century of family involvement in golf club manufacturing in St. Andrews.

Willie Auchterlonie (1872-1963) earned a niche in golfing history by winning the Open Golf Championship at Prestwick in 1893. From 1935 to 1963 he was Honorary Professional to the Royal and Ancient Golf Club. He was succeeded by his son Laurie, who held the post until his death in 1987. In 1964, Laurie turned the former premises of David and Willie Auchterlonie in Pilmuir Links, into an interesting museum of old golf clubs. Laurie also made a name for himself with golf associated work in the United States of America - in particular the establishment of a golfing museum at Foxburg.

23. Abbotsford Crescent

35

THE PANCAKE PLACE

PANCAKES GALORE
THE FAMILY RESTAURANT
WITH 100 SEATS &
BABY CHANGING FACILITIES
177-179 SOUTH STREET
ST. ANDREWS. tel. 475671
OPEN 7 DAYS - LICENSED

At the end of Golf Place there is a plaque to our right in Pilmuir Links on the house where Willie and Laurie Auchterlonie used to live and work. From the 1820's onwards the city started to expand westwards beyond the old city boundaries. The streets we will shortly walk through are part of this development. First of all we cross over Pilmuir Place and visit three streets which were the inspiration of James Hope. The layout consisted of Abbotsford Crescent, - a concave crescent, named after Sir Walter Scotts home in the Borders; Howard Place, a convex crescent, named after Hope's second wife and finally Hope Street, a straight street joining the other two. This development started in 1844 but was not finished until the 1890's.

At the end of Hope Street we cross over to the corner of Alexandra Place where we will see the Blue Stane in the gardens beyond the railings. This ancient stone may well have been a stone altar in the distant past. For many years the stone was often used as a meeting place and was held in great respect in more superstitious times.

On the other corner stands Hope Park Church, built in 1865 by Peddie & Kinnear. To our right, midway along Double Dykes Road, is the St. Andrews Museum at Kinburn House which opened in 1991. We now head for the West Port via St. Mary's Place and Bell Street.

In medieval times access to and from St. Andrews was controlled by Ports or Gateways. Formerly known as the Southgait, due to its original location further east, the West Port forms the main entrance to the old city of St. Andrews. The reconstruction of the West Port in 1589 was modelled on the old Netherbow Port in Edinburgh and today only the West Port survives. Further improvements in 1843 included a plaque on the west side of the main arch depicting the arms of David I, who granted permission to found the burgh of St. Andrews between 1144 and 1153. The City Arms are displayed on the eastern side of the Port and the two side arches were formed between 1843-45.

In 1650 Charles II was presented with the silver keys to the City at the Port. The next member of Royalty to be honoured in this way was the Prince of Wales, later to become King Edward VIII, when he received the freedom of the City in 1922 along with the Captaincy of the Royal and Ancient Golf Club.

Passing through the right hand gate or port there is a plaque which informs us of the history of the West Port. We now return to South Street — a wide tree lined avenue and one of the three main streets which converges on the Cathedral.

24. The West Port

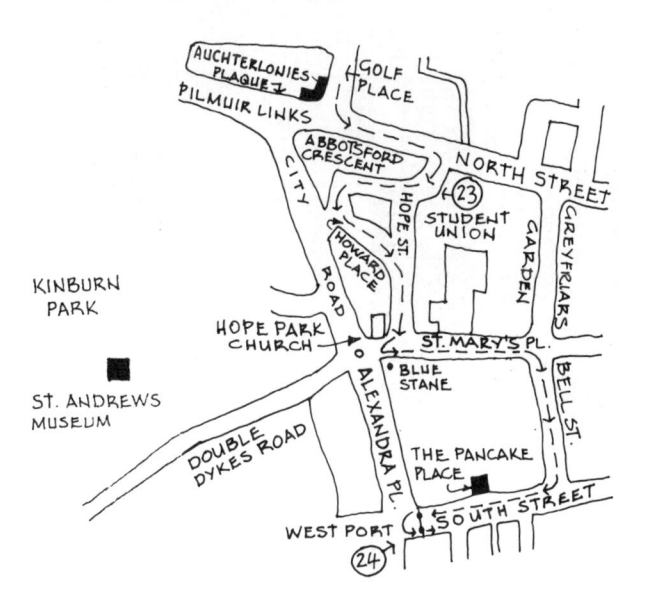

37

25. Louden's Close

Over to our right the Preservation Trust have restored no. 166 South Street. This house is another good example of Scottish burgh architecture of the 1800's, although the white harling covers the original stone. This is one of several buildings that has been renovated by the St. Andrews Preservation Trust which was founded in 1937. Its objectives are to preserve the amenities and historic character of St. Andrews by acquiring old buildings, and the Trust logo may be seen on several buildings throughout the town.

Cross over South Street and by pass Thistle Lane which still retains the old cobblestones of yesteryear. The houses either side of the lane run back at right angles to South Street. This formation is known as the Riggs and the best surviving example is that of Louden's Close, one of three closes sandwiched between Thistle Lane and Rose Lane. Before we visit Loudens Close, by pass Alison's Close with its metal gate, and take a detour into Imries Close where an old barn has been converted into a house. Prior to this the building was the first Secession Kirk of the Burghers in the town between 1749-74.

THE TRUST LOGO

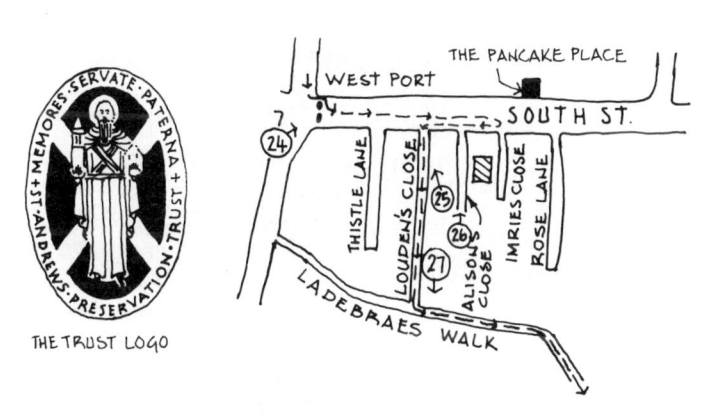

Returning to Loudens Close at no. 142-148 South Street we turn left through the pend. Immediately we have left behind the noisy, main street and find ourselves in a quite different environment hemmed in by the riggs as they run back along the line of the close. The cobbled edging, wall lamp, pantiled roof and dormers all capture the character of the old town.

Continue on along the close following the high stone dykes down towards the Lade Braes. Lade is Scots for a watercourse to a mill and brae is a steep hill. This walk starts near the Law Mill to the west of St. Andrews and follows the route of the Kinness Burn into town where the two diverge.

26. Alison's Close

27. Loudens Close leading to Ladebraes Walk.

28. Ladebraes Lane

We join the Lade Braes Walk as it twists and turns its way round the south boundary of Madras College. Hemmed in by the high stone dykes the way ahead is tantalisingly revealed, stage by stage, until the narrow lane turns abruptly into Ladebraes Lane and leads us into South Street. Here, we turn left and walk towards the remains of Blackfriars Chapel which stands in splendid isolation in front of Madras College.

29 Blackfriars Chapel

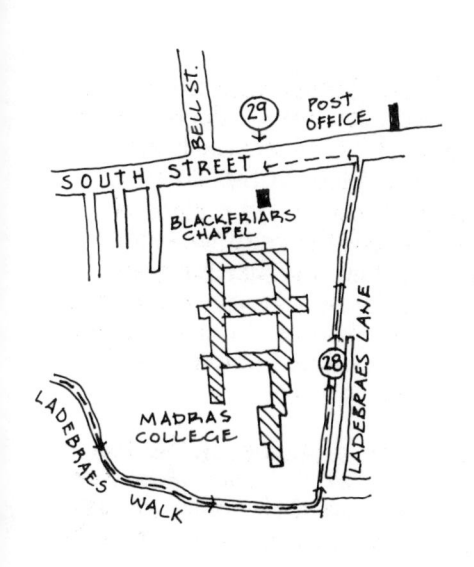

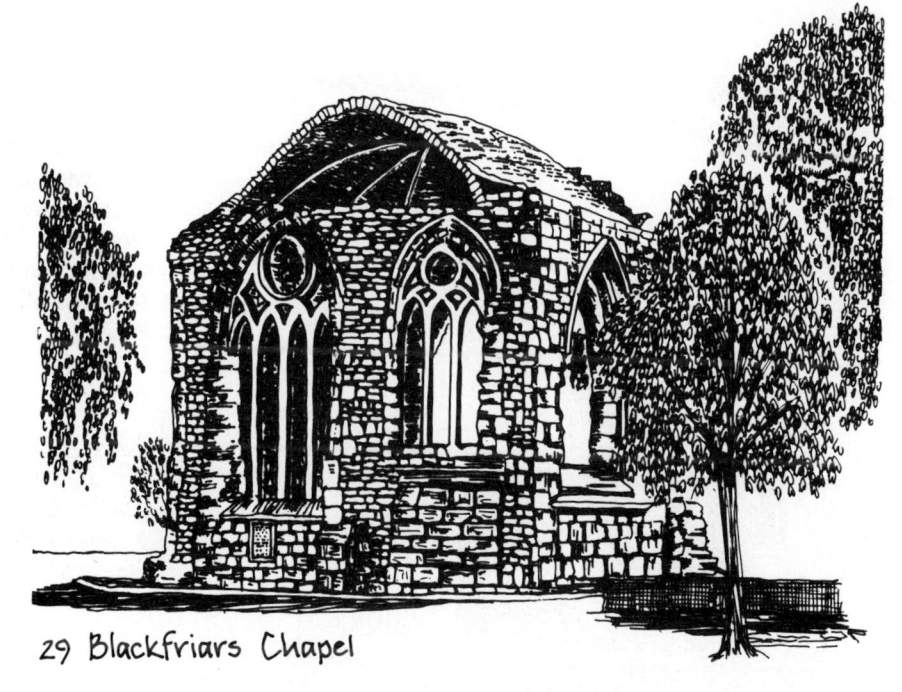

In 1525 the Chapel was added to the Blackfriars Monastery which was reputedly founded in the 1270's by Bishop Wishart. Following John Knox's famous sermon in 1559 the Monastery suffered greatly from the resultant rioting. Still visible on the underside of the vaulted roof are the signs of the crucifixion showing two hands, two feet, a spear piercing a heart, a dice box and three nails.

Madras College, was founded in 1832 with money donated by a native of St. Andrews - Dr. Andrew Bell. He was the son of Bailie Bell, of whom we will hear more later, and after graduating at St. Andrews University he was a missionary at Madras in India. After returning to his native Fife he established the College as a place for secondary education before progressing to University.

41

30. Burgher Close

Crossing over South Street keep a look out for Burgher Close. Its name derives from the Burgher Branch of the Secession Church who moved from Imrie Close in the 1770's to occupy one of the buildings as their place of worship. Ducking through the pend we enter a cobbled yard which contains another building successfully renovated by the Preservation Trust. A studio on the first floor houses Scotland's only Historical Research Illustration Establishment which is normally open to visitors.

Back out on South Street a plaque on the Post Office wall informs us that Dr. John Adamson (1809-1870) lived here from 1848-1865. He was a physician and pioneer photographer and he took the first calotype portrait in 1841.

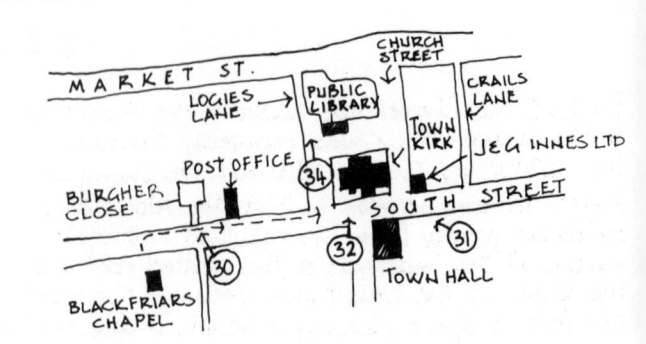

Further along South Street stands the Town Kirk of St. Andrews - the Holy Trinity Church. Built in 1410 this Kirk replaced an earlier one originally located near to the Cathedral. At the end of the eighteenth century the Kirk faced massive rebuilding and only the tower remains from the original building. This same tower often served as a prison for women who strayed from the straight and narrow path.

The main entry to the Kirk was built as a memorial to John Knox who preached his sermons from here in June 1559 to incite the congregation to take to the streets, and plunder the Cathedral and other religious buildings throughout St. Andrews.

Within the Kirk stand memorials to people who have featured largely in the history of the town. An impressive marble monument is dedicated to Archbishop James Sharp who met a cruel and bloody death on Magus Muir in 1679. Returning to St. Andrews the hated Archbishop was dragged from his stagecoach and butchered by a band of Covenanters. One of the leaders, Hackston of Rathillet, sat impassively on horse back and watched the whole proceedings. A year later, however, Hackston was executed in Edinburgh and parts of his body were displayed throughout Scotland as a warning to others.

31. The Town Kirk - Holy Trinity Church

The Archbishop's funeral service was conducted in the Town Kirk where he was buried, yet in 1849 when his tomb was opened there was no sign of his remains - only a broken coffin.

32. The Town Kirk - Holy Trinity Church

Other people commemorated in the Town Kirk include the Playfair family. The Playfair Aisle is to their memory. One family member directly associated with the Kirk is the Rev. Dr. Patrick Playfair. He was responsible for instigating the restoration work between 1907 and 1909. There is also a memorial to Old Tom Morris, the first Professional Golfer of the Royal and Ancient Golf Club and a staunch member of Holy Trinity Church.

The Town Kirk is steeped in history and contains many other noteworthy relics. One of them is the iron contraption known as the 'Bishop's Branks'. This was a crude framework which was attached to the head with a device which projected into the mouth thus rendering the unfortunate offender speechless. Legend has it that Archbishop Sharp instructed the 'Branks to be fitted to a certain Isobel Lindsay to silence her heckling during his sermon. Other relics are the three legged stools of repentance known as the Cutty Stools, the plate and six Communion cups presented by Archbishop Sharp and the tattered battalion flag of the 2nd Fifeshire Militia. There are many such items associated with the past history of St. Andrews within the Town Kirk which makes it a valuable museum to the town.

Opposite the Town Kirk is the Town Hall built in 1858 to replace the Old Tolbooth in Market Street. Built into the entry lobby is an old stone from the Tolbooth inscribed with the date 1565, and both the arms of Provost Sir Patrick Learmonth of Dairsie and the city of St. Andrews, excluding St. Andrew. At first floor level are the Main Hall and Council Chamber where there is a roll of all the Provosts dating way back to the first Provost in the twelfth century. The Provosts were appointed to control the administration of the burghs. Initially St. Andrews was a 'Burgh of Barony' or 'Bishop's Burgh' due to the presence of Bishop Robert (1126-1159). It also achieved the status of a Royal Burgh during the reign of David I (1124-1153) although the exact dates, in both cases, are somewhat vague.

PLAQUE ON CORNER TOWER OF TOWN HALL.

45

33. Town Hall

Hanging lantern & sign at J & G Innes Ltd.

Other ancient mementos of the Royal Burgh of St. Andrews are a wooden panel which displays the Arms of the City and is dated 1115; the original charter granted to St. Andrews by Malcolm IV; the executioner's axe; the City seals; a set of brass measures; the Provost's Chain of Office and a silver set of the Keys to the City which were presented to Charles II at the West Port in 1650.

On the outside wall facing Queen's Gardens is a mosaic designed by the Polish Forces who were stationed over here during the Second World War.

Located above the Town Hall are the premises of the Masonic Lodge of St. Andrew, no 25. The lodge dates back to 1600 but in those days the Masons met at the Black Bull Inn near Abbey Street. Prior to 1600 the masons were active in St. Andrews and many masons' marks are visible on the stonework in the ruined Cathedral which was built between the 12th - 14th century.

About 1830 the Lodge sold all its property and donated ten pounds to the Town Council. This allowed the Lodge to hold meetings in the Town Hall 'for all time coming'. At that time the Town Hall was located in Market Street and when the new Town Hall was built in South Street the Masons moved there in 1862. Although the Masons were allowed the use of the Council Chambers they campaigned for the use of the attic for their meetings. In the 1890's the attic was gifted to the Masons free of charge in perpetuity and the present temple was created in 1898. Of particular interest in the lodge is the painted elliptical dome ceiling with scenes of the world's famous architectural buildings. These are depicted in panoramic form around the base of the dome and include scenes of St. Andrews Cathedral. The dome was painted by Dundee artist Wilkie Gahan in 1904 and it is a mirror image of his eye that looks down on the scene of Jacob's ladder. The Lodge is open to the public on St. Andrew's Day.

Polish mosaic on Town Hall

47

At the corner of South Street and Church Street - formerly Kirk Wynd - stands a distinctive building. This was previously the offices of the St. Andrews Citizen which is the local paper dating from 1870 and still published today.

The business was purchased in 1879 by J & G Innes Ltd. and in 1927 the building was reconstructed by them in consultation with a local architect and craftsmen. The tudor style building has a natural charm and the shop stocks a very comprehensive range of stationery, books - especially children's books, traditional toys and games, table stationery and greeting cards.

Below the decorative corner turrets hangs a lantern with a plaque over the doorway telling the history of this site. The present building stands on the site of the house of Bailie Bell, father of Andrew Bell who founded Madras College. Bailie was a local barber with a flair for watchmaking and machinery and he worked alongside Alexander Wilson in perfecting a system of type founding. This system was accepted and consequently Wilson was acknowledged as the father of Scottish Type-Founding. Bailie Bell was also associated with John Baine whose type foundry in Philadelphia cast the first $ sign in 1797.

J & G Innes Ltd.
107, South Street, St. Andrews
tel. 01334 472174

Another link with the United States of America is with James Wilson, (1742-1798) who was born at Carskerdo, by St. Andrews. Wilson attended St. Andrews University before emigrating to North America in 1765. Eventually he gained the post of Professor of English Literature at the College of Philadelphia. He was directly involved in the preparation of the Treaty of American Declaration of Independence in 1776.

The character of buildings is always enhanced by decorative features and symbols. On the Town Hall, for example, there are plaques and a mosaic panel; at the corner of South Street and Logie's Lane there is a larger than life mortar and pestle; the Town Kirk is surrounded by decorative wrought iron gates and railings and across the street there are eyecatching hanging signs and a lantern on the J. & G. Innes building. All of these individual features contribute to the character of both the buildings and street scene.

Leaving South Street momentarily we proceed down Logie's Lane with the domestic scale of the two storey housing emphasising the massive bulk of the Town Kirk. The lane narrows as we near the pend and once through we enter into Market Street. Turn right and head towards the old market area where the Tolbooth stood until demolished in 1862.

34 Logie's Lane

It was from this same Tolbooth that part of the body of Hackston of Rathillet was hung after he was executed for his role in the murder of Archbishop Sharp. The Tolbooth and Old Town Hall were located near the west end of Market Street thus forming a square. The focal point of the square was the Mercat Cross which was removed in 1768 and its site is marked by a red cobbled cross in the road. The colour of the cross is perhaps symbolic of the atrociously cruel executions that took place near the Mercat Cross over the centuries.

Two of the more notable executions included that of the Bohemian, Paul Craw, who was slowly burned to death in 1433 for his religious beliefs. On the instructions of Bishop Wardlaw, the same man that helped found the University, a brass ball was forced into Craw's mouth to prevent him preaching to the crowd. The other execution was that of Chastelard who was beheaded in 1563 for venturing into Queen Mary's bedroom.

Today the focal point in Market Place is the Whyte-Melville Memorial Fountain which was erected in memory of the novelist George Whyte-Melville who was killed while hunting.

35 Looking down College Street to St. Salvator's Tower

50

The fountain is also the focal point for an ancient weekly farm and garden produce market which takes place every Saturday. Moving on and glancing left down College Street we glimpse the stone spire of St. Salvators towering over the houses below. As we continue on down Market Street the road narrows and the view ahead is cut off by a typical two storey traditional house in South Castle Street. Excluding the modern block to our left Market Street has a traditional domestic character enhanced by the crowstep gables, dormers and local building materials.

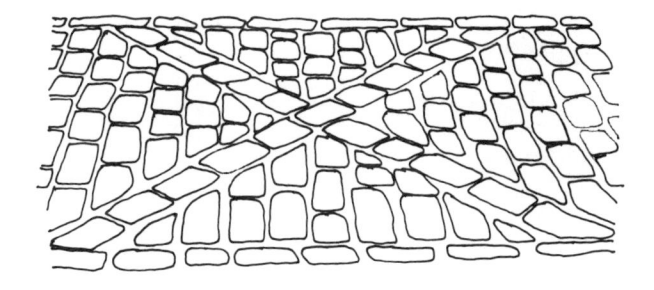

Site of the old Mercat Cross

36. The Whyte-Melville Memorial Fountain

51

Keep an eye open for one such traditional stone gable as it is just past here that we turn right into Crails Lane which links up with South Street. Crails Lane is a good example of a wynd - Scots for a narrow lane. This lane has a certain attractiveness which is enhanced with hanging signs, an old street lamp and an overhanging tree which obscures a complete view to the other end. Look out for the simple old shoe scraper tucked into the stone wall by a doorstep. As the lane curves left and then narrows we catch a glimpse of the close at the far end which is not fully revealed until the last moment. It is only then that we see the close framing the entry to St. Mary's College on the far side of South Street.

37 Crails Lane

Shoe scraper

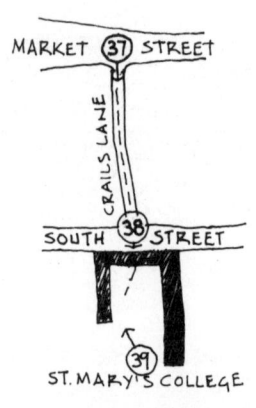

The metal gateway allows us to see through the arched entrance into the courtyard beyond giving us a glimpse of what we will encounter. The coat of arms combines both the arms of Archbishops James Beaton and John Hamilton and the motto below is from St. John's Gospel.-'In the beginning was the word.' On passing through the arch the massive Holm Oak seems to engulf the whole courtyard. This oak tree was planted in 1728 but is relatively young compared to the ancient thorn tree over to our right at the foot of the Bell-tower. This thorn tree was reputedly planted by Mary Queen of Scots in the mid-sixteenth century making it about four hundred and fifty years old.

St. Mary's College was founded in 1537 by Archbishop James Beaton and built on the site of the Old St. John's Pedagogy of 1430. The new buildings were completed in 1554 under the authority of Archbishop John Hamilton and the north and west buildings still stand today. The College was originally established for 'the teaching of the Catholic faith but after 1559 it became the main centre for Protestant tuition in Scotland.

38. Entrance to St. Mary's College

39 The Quadrangle at St. Mary's College

Taking the right hand path we walk on past the Bell Tower, the ancient thorn tree, a sundial dating back to 1664 and the ruins of the fifteenth century St. John's Gate. At the foot of the Long Walk is an eighteenth century ivy covered doocot. Throughout the east neuk of Fife the doocots are a familar sight and long ago the doos or pigeons made a tasty meal in the long winter months when food was scarce. Over on the east side was the site of the Old University Library Founded by James IV in 1612.

It was completed in 1643 and two years later the Lower Hall was the meeting place for the Scottish Estates and ever since has been known as Parliament Hall. Throughout the next three hundred years various alterations and extensions took place and in 1976 the University built a new library over in North Street. The Old Library houses many treasures including a clock dated 1672 which was made to help James Gregory, the inventor of the Gregorian Telescope, with his astronomical calculations.

Royal Arms of Scotland

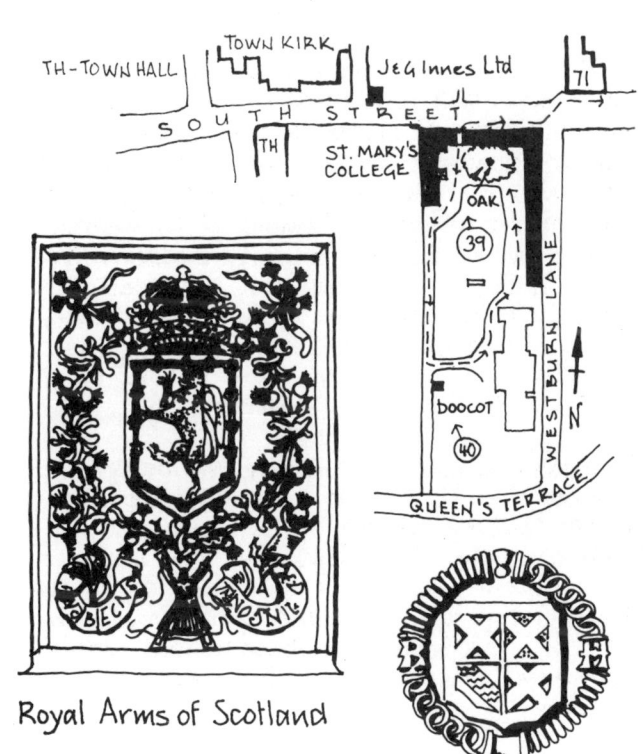

On leaving St. Mary's College we turn right into South Street. High up on this facade are the Arms of most of the Chancellors of the University dating back to that of Henry Wardlaw in 1411. There are also the Royal Arms of Scotland with the figure of St. Andrew and the date 1563.

40. The Doocot

55

This section of South Street is of particular interest and both sides of the street are good examples of sixteenth and seventeenth century domestic town architecture. Located over several of the doorways are the coats of arms of the influential families of St. Andrews. Before Baker Lane, formerly Baxters Wynd, is no. 71 South Street which is the oldest property in the burgh. As we have noted many of the streets and wynds have been anglicised and with each change of name a little bit of the town heritage is chipped away.

On a gable in Baker Lane are the battered features of a Crusader — a reminder of the twelfth century Knights of St. John who featured in the Crusades in the Holy Lands. The militant Knights Templar led to their own downfall through greed and corruption and by 1309 their properties had been handed over to the Knight Hospitallers of the same order of St. John.

With their massive wealth the Knights acquired property in both Edinburgh and St. Andrews, and 71 South Street was one of their largest properties. Today the property is owned by the University and is appropriately used by the Department of Medieval History.

41. No 71 South Street

We continue along South Street looking out for the hanging sign indicating the Byre Theatre, and alongside is one of the family coat of arms. The framed view through this close is quite enticing. Straightahead a wide flight of steps with decorative iron railings catches the eye. The way ahead, however, is hinted at by a glimpse through the close in the corner. The stone slabs emphasise this route as they form a path through the cobbled setts. In springtime the tree blossom provides a splendid splash of colour.

Coats of arms on 40 South St.

The battered head

Entry to South Court

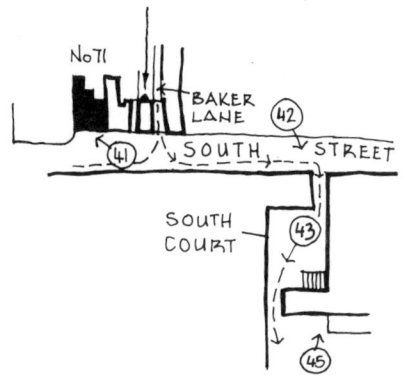

43. South Court

57

This doocot was taken from the old byre and built into the Abbey St. Frontage of the new Byre Theatre.

44. The Byre Theatre

On reaching this far close we can see the new Byre Theatre. Byre is Scots for cowshed and the original theatre performances took place in an old Byre of the Abbey Dairy Farm. This fifteen metre long by four metre wide converted byre had a seating capacity of seventy three. The first private performance took place in 1933 with members of the St. Andrews Play Club under the guidance of Alex. Paterson. MBE.

Two years later the Byre was licensed as a public theatre. The cramped conditions created a unique atmosphere for both audience and actors, and the latter were often involved in many unusual 'behind the scenes' acts only peculiar to the Byre. An actor, for instance, who left the stage on one side to enter on the other had to go outside, climb an external stair, sprachle through the loft then re-enter via another stair on to the stage.

Eventually various pressures including plans for development of Abbey Street, constrained audience and acting conditions and ever increasing maintenance costs brought about demands for a new theatre. Consequently the old Byre Theatre was demolished in 1967 and the new theatre opened in 1970. Further development is now planned and by 1998 the latest Byre will house a theatre with over 220 seats, a theatre workshop, offices and a restaurant.

Even today the Byre Theatre is the only place in St. Andrews which is licensed as a theatre. The Byre supports a small core of full time professional actors ably backed by enthusiastic and talented amateurs. A popular feature of the Byre policy has always been to present local plays which have a Fife flavour.

Byre Theatre

45. South Court, a 16th century mansion.

59

46. The Roundel

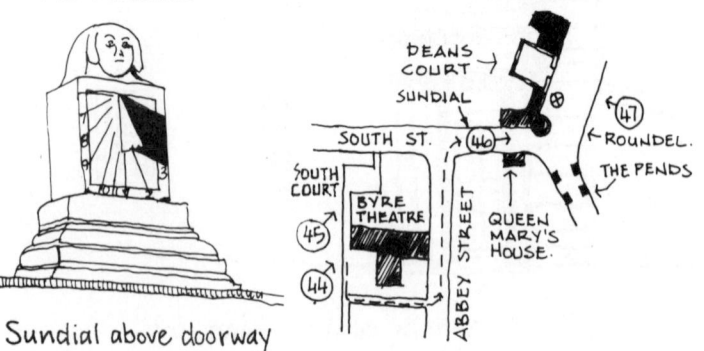

Sundial above doorway

Continue on down past the Byre Theatre turning left and left again into Abbey Street, formerly Priors Wynd. Across the road we see another section of the Abbey Wall with one of its many towers. This particular tower was moved to allow road widening improvements to the street.

At the corner of Abbey Street and South Street we are once again within the vicinity of the Cathedral. The houses on the north side of South Street continue to reflect the traditional qualities of domestic architecture of the sixteenth and seventeenth century. This row of houses terminates on the corner with the eyecatching Roundel. This round tower is an interesting townscape feature with its arched doorway and stone balustrading.

On this side of the street stand an excellent restored example of a seventeenth century merchants house at no 24. The only other house of note is where Mary Queen of Scots stayed on her visit to St. Andrews in 1564. During a previous visit the French courtier, Chastelard burst into the Queens bedroom. This impetuous behaviour cost him his life and after a public trial he was executed at the Mercat Cross.

On rounding the corner we are now in front of Deans Court, a sixteenth century building on the site of the old Archdeacons residence. Today Deans Court is used as a Hall of Residence for the University. In front of the archway a cross within a circle is clearly marked out in the cobbled pavement. This was where Walter Myln, an eighty year old Lutherian Priest, was burned at the stake in 1558 on the orders of Archbishop John Hamilton. He too died a violent death and was executed in 1571 for his involvement in the murder of Lord Darnley, Mary Queen of Scots second husband.

Above the iron gateway are the arms of George Douglas of Loch Leven who ably assisted Mary Queen of Scots in her escape from the Island Castle on Loch Leven in 1568. In the centre of the courtyard stands a well and in the far distance is the spire of St. Salvators Tower.

47. Deans Court

From Deans Court we slip down Gregorys Lane to the East Scores. Turning right we then follow the cliff path down to the Abbey Wall and in the shadow of St Rules Tower and the ruined Cathedral this leads us to where it all started on...........

Kirkhill

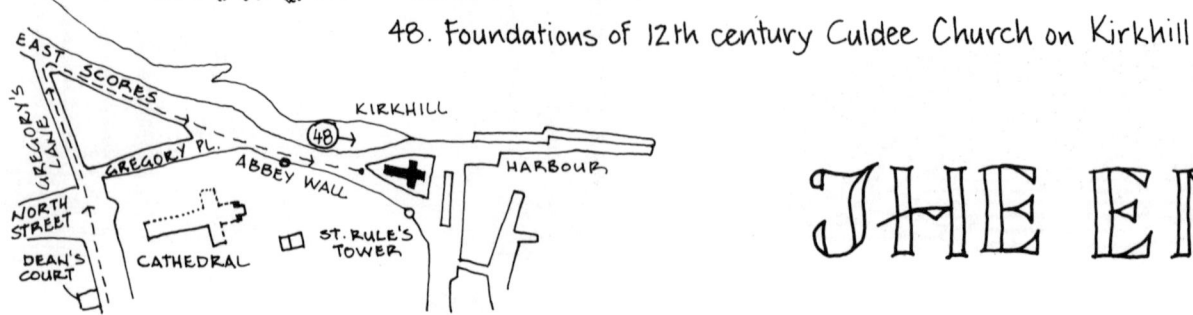

48. Foundations of 12th century Culdee Church on Kirkhill

THE END

BIBLIOGRAPHY

About St. Andrews and about by James K. Robertson
A Visitor's Guide to St. Andrews and the East Neuk by R. Lamont-Brown
Discovering Old St. Andrews - St Andrew Society of St. Andrews
Golf legends by Angus G Garber
Hay Flemings Abridged Guide to St Andrews
Shadows of St Andrews Past by David W Lyle
St Andrews Castle by Stewart Cruden
St Andrews Cathedral by Stewart Cruden
St. Andrews City of Change by R. Lamont-Brown & P. Adamson
St. Andrews - The Guide and handbook of the St. Andrews Preservation Trust
The Kingdom of Fife and Kinross-shire by Theo Lang
The Buildings of Scotland - Fife by John Gifford.
Trade Reminiscences & History of Lodge St Andrew, no 25.

PROVOST'S LAMP OUTSIDE TOWN HALL

PLAQUE FROM ST. MARY'S COLLEGE

COAT OF ARMS OF ONE OF THE CHANCELLORS OF THE UNIVERSITY.

MORTAR & PESTLE

For a black and white, pen and ink sketch of your house or a pen and ink sketch tinted with watercolour

contact: John Pearson
'Lingmoor', Carberry Park, Leven, Fife.
tel. 01333·426248 / 01738 635118.

Other publications by John M. Pearson

A Guided Walk round Inverness
A Guided Walk round Edinburgh
Edinburgh Old Town Pilgrims' Way - (text by Donald Smith)
Series on Districts in Fife:-
'Around North East Fife'
Around Kirkcaldy
Around Dunfermline"
Burntisland
Around Stirling
Around Perthshire
Maps: St. Andrews Street Map.
Edinburgh - Royal Mile Guide
& Old Town Pilgrims Way.

The Author:

John MacMillan Pearson was born at St. Andrews in 1952. He is an architect by profession having graduated with a Bachelor of Architecture degree at Heriot-Watt University, Edinburgh in 1976. Travelled overseas between 1977-1983 to Canada, Mexico and the Far East and worked in New Zealand and Australia before returning to Scotland. Developed a keen interest in sketching and calligraphy through meeting the Canadian artist Barbara Elizabeth Mercer. From 1983-1987 he worked for the Edinburgh architects' firm, Dick Peddie & McKay at their branch office in Invergordon. Following a six year spell in London area, while working on an office development for Grosvenor Developments at Harrow, he returned to Scotland in 1993 and is now based at Perth working on a freelance basis.